BEGINNING HISTORY

VICTORIAN CHILDREN

Anne Steel

Illustrated by Bernard Long

BEGINNING HISTORY

Crusaders
Egyptian Pyramids
Greek Cities
Medieval Markets
Norman Castles
Roman Soldiers
Saxon Villages
Tudor Sailors
Victorian Children
Viking Explorers

All words that appear in **bold** are explained in the glossary on page 22.

Series editor: Catherine Ellis
Book editor: Clare Chandler
Designer: Helen White

First published in 1989 by Wayland (Publishers) Limited,
61 Western Road, Hove, East Sussex BN3 1JD.

© Copyright 1989 Wayland (Publishers) Ltd

British Library Cataloguing in Publication Data
Steel, Anne
Victorian children.
1. Great Britain. Social life, 1837–1901
I. Title   II. Long, Bernard   III. Series
941.081'088054

ISBN 1–85210–816–9

Typeset by Kalligraphics Limited, Horley, Surrey.
Printed in Italy by G.Canale & C.S.p.A., Turin.
Bound in Belgium by Casterman. S.A.

CONTENTS

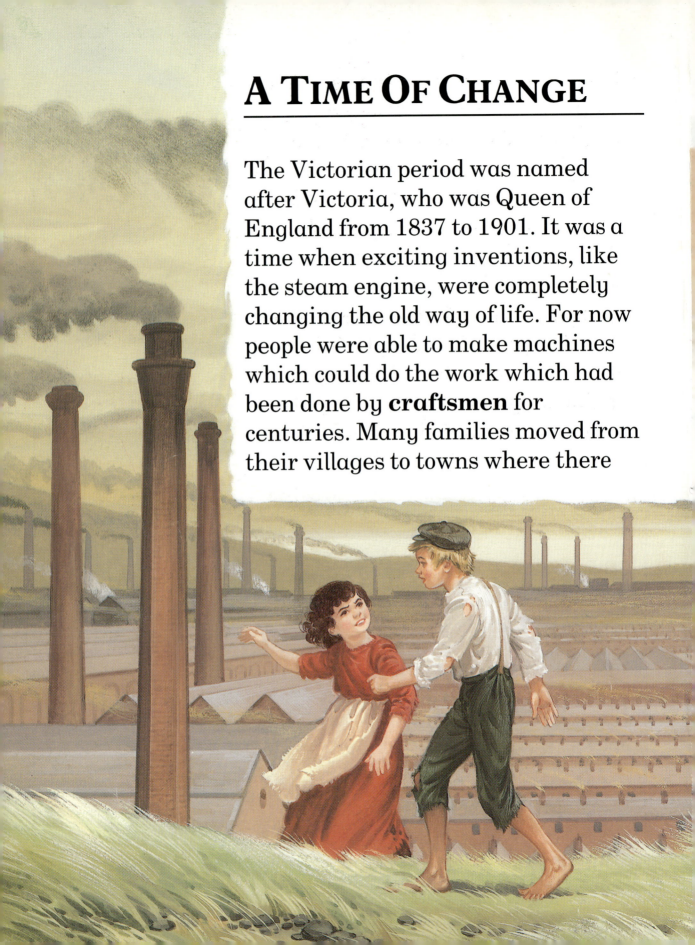

A TIME OF CHANGE

The Victorian period was named after Victoria, who was Queen of England from 1837 to 1901. It was a time when exciting inventions, like the steam engine, were completely changing the old way of life. For now people were able to make machines which could do the work which had been done by **craftsmen** for centuries. Many families moved from their villages to towns where there

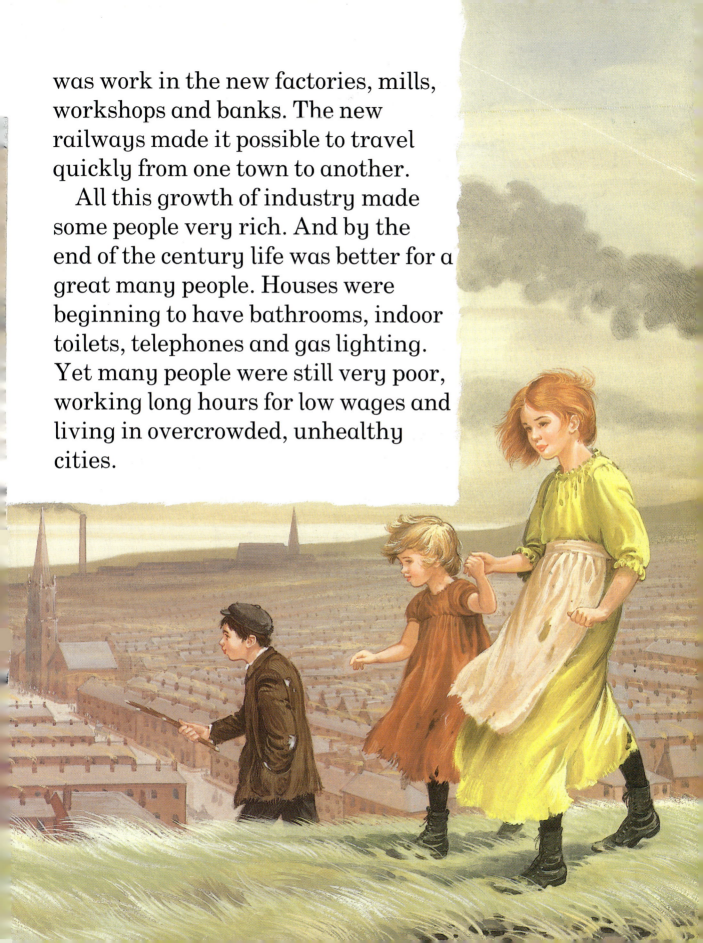

was work in the new factories, mills, workshops and banks. The new railways made it possible to travel quickly from one town to another.

All this growth of industry made some people very rich. And by the end of the century life was better for a great many people. Houses were beginning to have bathrooms, indoor toilets, telephones and gas lighting. Yet many people were still very poor, working long hours for low wages and living in overcrowded, unhealthy cities.

CITY LIFE

In the busy, overcrowded cities, many poor families lived in **slums**. The houses were built quickly and cheaply for the factory workers. There were no gardens and children had to play in the narrow, dirty spaces between the tall buildings. Families were often very large, sometimes with ten or more children.

Children queueing to collect water from the only tap in the street.

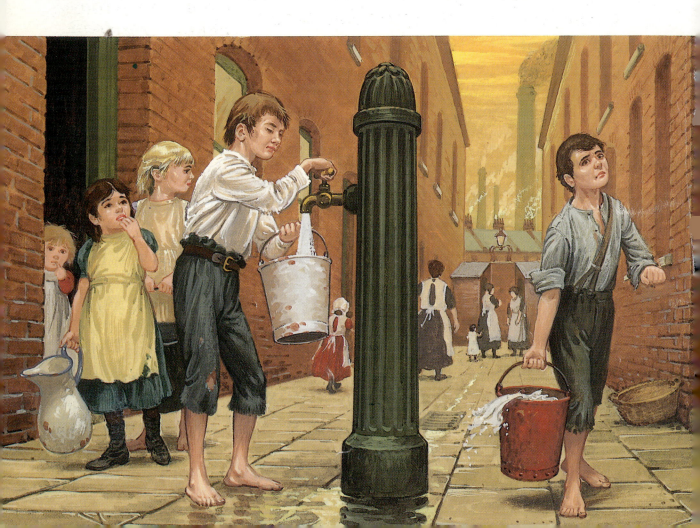

All the children might have to share one bed, sleeping at both ends.

Inside, the houses were often damp and stale-smelling, as fresh air was thought to be unhealthy. People did not wash much, as everyone in the area had to share one outside tap. The water was often **polluted**. They also shared one outside toilet.

dirty smelly, unhealthy

These people had a bad diet, usually of bread and **dripping**, cheese, bacon and tea. They were poorly dressed and the children often went barefoot. The conditions made people unhealthy, and many young children died from fevers, **smallpox**, measles or **tuberculosis**.

fat from meat

disease fever & spots

lung disease

Children watch as a 'climbing boy' clambers up the chimney to clean out the soot.

COUNTRY LIFE

Most country families worked for the local landowner, living in small cottages on his land. Other families lived in their own homes in the village, where the men worked as **blacksmiths**, **cobblers**, millers and brewers.

The children worked in the home, the workshop, and on the land, especially at harvest time. They were given special jobs like collecting the ears of corn left behind by the harvesters when the crop had been cut and gathered into **sheaves**. Children also collected firewood, fed animals, brought water from the

Above *This boy is keeping the birds away from the crops with his wooden bird-scarer.*

Right *Country children taking a rest from their chores to play 'Ring-a-ring-o-roses'.*

pump or well, scared birds away from the growing crops and caught rats and mice. They picked hops for beer making, wild flowers for wine and gathered acorns for the pigs to eat.

Life was hard for the children, as many families were very poor. But they did have fresh air, and fields, woods and streams to play in. So they were generally healthier and happier than children from the city slums.

Children gathering the ears of corn left by the harvesters.

LIVING IN A WEALTHY FAMILY

Wealthy families lived in the countryside, or on the edges of the cities, where there were parks, fields and cleaner air.

The father was the head of the family. Often he was feared by his children, his servants and his wife, who were all expected to obey him. The children had to be well-behaved at all times, and were taught only to speak when they were spoken to

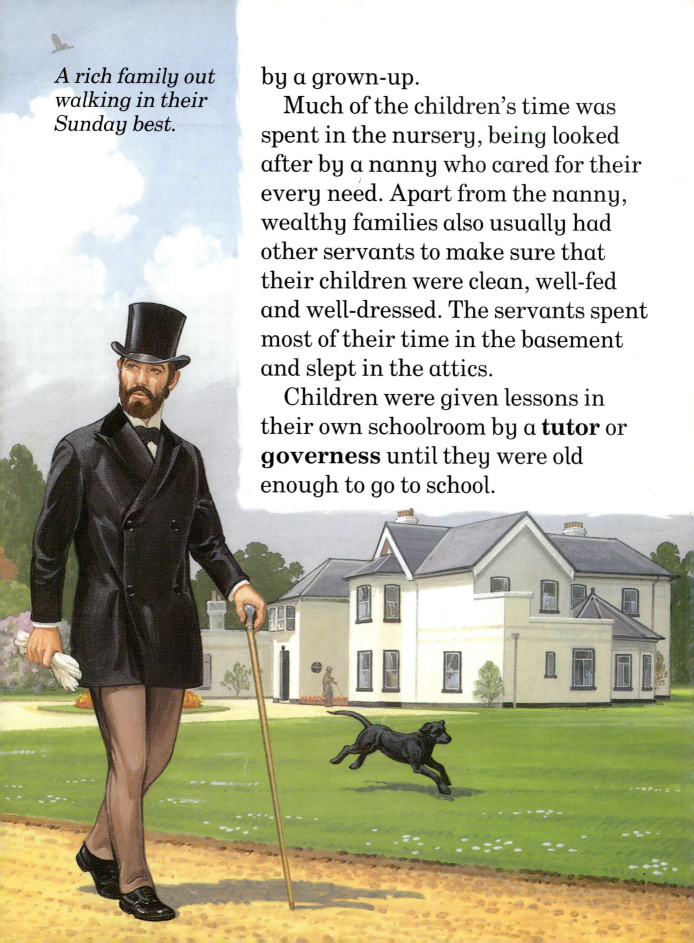

A rich family out walking in their Sunday best.

by a grown-up.

Much of the children's time was spent in the nursery, being looked after by a nanny who cared for their every need. Apart from the nanny, wealthy families also usually had other servants to make sure that their children were clean, well-fed and well-dressed. The servants spent most of their time in the basement and slept in the attics.

Children were given lessons in their own schoolroom by a **tutor** or **governess** until they were old enough to go to school.

CHILDREN AT WORK

Many children had to work to help their families earn enough money to live. Employers used them as cheap labour. Some eight or nine-year-olds worked a twelve hour day in factories and mills, doing boring and dangerous jobs like sweeping dust from under machines.

Many children worked underground in the coal mines, where they were

Right *Children often worked in noisy and dangerous factories.*

Below *These young boys worked all day in the dark coal mines.*

small enough to drag trucks of coal along the narrow tunnels. Children as young as five worked in the tunnels opening doors to let the trucks through. This was dangerous work, and there were often accidents.

Chimney sweeps used young boys to climb chimneys and clean away the soot. They were often burned or hurt. By the end of Victorian times, laws had been passed to stop young children working in the factories and mines, and chimney sweeps were no longer allowed to use boys.

Below *A chimney sweep with his boy, ready for work.*

SCHOOLS

Until 1870 there was no law to make parents send their children to school. Some poor children went to **charity schools**, where they paid two pence a week, but many worked instead. After 1870 all children between five and thirteen had to go to school. They were taught reading, writing, arithmetic and **scripture** in classes with as many as 80 pupils.

The teacher was very strict and used a cane. The lessons were often boring, with much chanting of spellings and tables, and copying in sand trays and on slates. Many pupils

This governess taught the girls from a wealthy family at home.

had to share reading books.

Boys from wealthy families went to one of the large public schools, such as Eton, Harrow or Winchester. There were fewer schools for the girls, as it was not thought important for them to go to school. Their future was to look after a household. They were taught good manners and how to move gracefully, and learned reading, sewing, music, dancing and drawing.

These children are learning their times tables by heart, under the stern eye of the teacher.

GAMES AND TOYS

Victorian children enjoyed party games which we still play today, like 'Hunt the Slipper', 'Blind Man's Buff' and charades. They played card games such as 'Happy Families' and 'Beat Your Neighbour'.

Wealthy children read books like *Black Beauty*, *Treasure Island*, *Alice in Wonderland* and *The Water Babies*. They also read comics, but there were not as many different ones

as we have today. One of the favourites was called *The Little Folks*.

Most toys belonged to children from wealthy families. Popular ones were wooden rocking horses and dolls' houses, lead and tin soldiers and wax-faced dolls. Outdoor games included hopscotch, marbles, skipping, football and playing with hoops and tops. Poor children who did not have any marbles played in the street with buttons and stones. They sometimes played football with a bundle of rags instead of a real leather ball.

THE WORKHOUSE

Very poor families or orphans might have to enter a workhouse where they were fed and given a bed. Families were split up and were only allowed one hour together on a Sunday afternoon.

There were strict rules about behaviour, doing chores and keeping clean. Disobedient children were fed on bread and water for a day or two,

Children being given a meal of gruel in the workhouse.

instead of the usual **gruel**. Unhappy children often ran away, but they were usually caught and punished.

There were lessons in the workhouse, so that the children would be able to find a job when they were old enough to leave. Some children were **fostered** by families if they were well-behaved.

Many orphans would not go into a workhouse. They lived on the streets and in empty buildings, and made a living by sweeping the streets, begging or thieving. Some formed groups of pickpockets.

The very poor went into the workhouse to avoid starvation and homelessness.

ENTERTAINMENTS

Everyone enjoyed a day out at the local fair, with its swings, roundabouts, sideshows, wrestling and boxing. The circus was another favourite treat, and people lined the streets to watch the wagons and animals march through the town to the circus site.

Many families liked watching football and cricket, or enjoyed spending a day at the races. Dog-fighting was another popular sport,

which is now thought to be cruel. Country children enjoyed festivals such as the **harvest-home** when the harvest was brought in, and **May Day** celebrations.

More and more people began to have day trips and holidays at the seaside. They travelled on the new railways to places like Brighton, Margate and Blackpool, to get away from city life for a short while.

Workhouse children hardly ever had any treats, but they might sometimes be taken for a walk to have a picnic in the local park.

GLOSSARY

Blacksmith A person who makes things from iron.

Charity schools Schools for poor children, often paid for by the Church.

Cobbler A person who mends shoes.

Craftsmen People who make things with their hands, not by machine.

Dripping The fat that drips from meat during cooking.

Fostered Looked after and brought up by people who are not the child's real parents.

Governess A woman who taught children in their own home.

Gruel A liquid food made from oatmeal and water.

Harvest-home Festival to celebrate the harvest.

May Day The first day of May.

Polluted Made dirty and unhealthy.

Scripture The study of the Bible.

Sheaves Stalks of corn tied up in bundles.

Slums The overcrowded, poor parts of a city.

Smallpox A disease which causes a fever and spots which can leave scars.

Tuberculosis A lung disease.

Tutor A man who taught children in their own home.

BOOKS TO READ

The Machine Makers by F. Lawton (Macdonald, 1975).

The Poor in Nineteenth Century Britain by M. Jones (Batsford, 1986).

Queen Anne to Queen Victoria by R. J. Unstead (A & C Black, 1974).

The Victorians by Miriam Moss (Wayland, 1986).

Victorian Britain by Tony Triggs (Wayland, 1990).

Victorian Children by Eleanor Allen (A. & C. Black, 1973).

Victorian Towns by M. Rawcliffe (Batsford, 1982).

Picture Acknowledgements

Aldus Archive 13 (top), 14; Bridgeman Art Library 7, 8 (bottom), 13 (bottom), 19; Mary Evans Picture Library 8 (top).

INDEX